Who's Who

in the
Bible

Claire Llewellyn

KING*f*ISHER

NEW YORK

Editor: Hannah Wilson
Design: Mike Buckley and Jane Tassie
Production Controller: Jo Blackmore
DTP Manager: Nicky Studdart
Artwork Archivists: Wendy Allison and Steve Robinson

Special thanks to our Bible Consultant, Annette Reynolds at AD Publishing Services

The publishers would like to thank the following artists for their contribution to this book:

Harry Bishop; Gino D'Achille (*Artist Partners Ltd.*); Richard Garland; Rob Hefferan (*Advocate*);
John Keay; Michael Langham Rowe; Massimiliano Longo (*Milan Illustrations Agency*);
Kevin Maddison; Chris Molan; Rob Perry (*Advocate*); Francis Phillipps;
Martin Reiner; Nick Spender (*Advocate*); Roger Stewart

KINGFISHER
a Houghton Mifflin Company imprint
215 Park Avenue South
New York, New York 10003
www.houghtonmifflinbooks.com

First published in 2002
2 4 6 8 10 9 7 5 3 1
1TR/0502/TWP/FR(FR)/150SMA

LIBRARY OF CONGRESS CATALOGING-IN-PUBLICATION DATA
has been applied for.

ISBN 0-7534-5456-4

Printed in Malaysia

Contents

Introduction

The Bible contains many wonderful stories about all kinds of people—kings, queens, soldiers, prophets, and ordinary men and women. Some of these people are weak and wicked, and others are generous and strong. This book tells their stories.

The stories follow the order of the Bible—roughly the order in which the events are thought to have happened. So if you don't know much about the Bible, read from the beginning to find out the whole story. But if you want to find out about particular people, find their names in the index on pages 62 and 63. If you come across a word you don't understand, look it up in the glossary on page 64.

Some stories in the Bible are sad. They are about illness, anger, punishment, and death. Others are full of love, courage, and faith. All have an important purpose, strengthening people's faith in God.

Places in the Bible

TURKEY

GREECE
ITALY

Mediterranean Sea

•Damascus

CANAAN

EGYPT

Mt. Sinai ▲

Nile River

Red Sea

•Haran •Nineveh

ASSYRIA

MESOPOTAMIA

BABYLONIA •Babylon

PERSIA

Mediterranean Sea

Capernaum Sea of Galilee

Nazareth• GALILEE
Shunem•

ISRAEL

Jordan River

Shiloh•

•Joppa

Jericho•
•Emmaus

Jerusalem•

Bethlehem• Dead Sea

•Hebron

JUDEA MOAB

Sodom•

THE LAND ONCE CALLED CANAAN

The people in these stories lived
in Egypt and the countries we
now call Israel, Jordan, Turkey,
Syria, Iraq, and Iran. Of course
place names and borders
change over the years, but the maps on this page provide
a basic guide to the area. When you come across a place
name, such as Canaan or Judea, in a particular story,
look at these maps to discover where the events took place.

God

In the beginning God created the universe. Before that there was nothing but darkness and swirling waters.

On the first day God made day and night. On the second day God made the sky. On the third day God made the sea and the land and ordered plants to grow. On the fourth day God made the sun, moon, and stars. On the fifth day God filled the seas with fish and the skies with birds. On the sixth day God created all the animals on the land and men and women too. Now the creation was complete, and on the seventh day God rested.

God was pleased with the creation, and He loves and cares about earth and all its many creatures.

From time to time God has appeared to people— sometimes as a column of fire or as thunder or as a flash of lightning. God appeared to Moses as a burning bush. But most of all, God appeared in person as Jesus.

God looks after the creation in three different ways— as the Father who made human beings and loves them; as the Son, Jesus, who died to save people from their sins and then rose again; and as the Holy Spirit who gives power to human beings, allowing them to live holy lives. In these ways God loves and cares for every living creature.

Adam and Eve

Adam and Eve were the first people to be created by God. God put them in a beautiful garden full of wonderful fruit trees in a land called Eden.

God told Adam and Eve to take care of all the living things in the Garden of Eden. God said they could eat any fruit in the garden except the fruit from the Tree of Knowledge. If they ate this, they would die.

An evil snake tempted Adam and Eve to taste the forbidden fruit, telling them that it would make them wise. The moment Adam and Eve ate the fruit they saw that they were naked. God soon discovered what they had done and was angry at their disobedience. God clothed them in animal skins and told them they had to leave the garden. From then on Adam and Eve had to work hard to feed themselves until the day they died.

Cain and Abel

Adam and Eve had two sons who were named Cain and Abel. The two men were different and had different jobs. Cain liked to grow crops, but Abel preferred to raise sheep.

They were both successful in their jobs, so Cain and Abel wanted to thank God by offering Him a gift. Abel sacrificed his firstborn lamb. Cain offered a bundle of wheat. God saw into Abel's heart and accepted his gift. God saw into Cain's heart and did not accept his gift. This made Cain so jealous and angry that he killed his brother.

When God asked Cain where Abel was, Cain pretended not to know. But God knew that he had murdered his brother and so cursed him.

Cain could never grow crops again and had to wander the earth alone.

Noah

Noah lived at a time when people were so wicked that God decided to destroy everyone. But Noah was a good man, and God wanted to save him. God told Noah to build an ark, a huge boat, that was big enough to hold all of his family and two of every kind of creature. Noah obeyed.

When all were on the ark, it started to rain. It rained for 40 days and 40 nights. Floodwater covered the earth, and every living creature drowned.

When the rain stopped, Noah sent a dove from the ark. It returned with an olive branch in its beak. Noah knew that the water had gone down and that he could leave the ark soon. God promised that the earth would never be flooded again and sent a rainbow as a sign of this promise.

Abraham

When Abraham was an old man living in Haran, God told him to take his family to the land of Canaan, promising that he would become the father of a great nation. Abraham set off on the long journey with his wife, Sarah, and eventually they settled in Hebron, in Canaan.

In time Sarah gave birth to a son and named him Isaac. Many years later God decided to test Abraham by asking him to kill Isaac as a sacrifice. Abraham loved Isaac, but he trusted God and wanted to obey the order. Just as he was about to kill the boy on a mountaintop an angel sent by God stopped him. Abraham sacrificed a ram instead.

God had tested Abraham's faith and knew that it was strong. God blessed him, his son, and all of his descendants—the nation of people who later were known as the Israelites.

Lot

Lot was Abraham's nephew. He had traveled to Canaan with Abraham and Sarah, but he had settled in a place called Sodom, not far from the city of Gomorrah.

The people of Sodom and Gomorrah were very wicked, and God decided to destroy them. But first God sent two angels to Sodom. Lot invited them into his house, and the angels warned him to leave the city because it was about to be destroyed. They led Lot, his wife, and their two daughters out of Sodom and ordered them not to look back.

Suddenly balls of fire and burning stones rained down on Sodom and Gomorrah. Lot and his daughters hurried to safety, but his wife took one last look behind her. She had disobeyed the angels and was turned into a pillar of salt.

Isaac and Rebecca

Isaac was the son of Abraham and Sarah. When Isaac was a young man, Abraham wanted to find a wife for him—someone who came from Mesopotamia, the land of his birth. So he asked a servant to travel there to find one. The servant's task was very important, and Abraham explained that God would guide him. So the servant set off for Abraham's birthplace.

When he arrived in Mesopotamia, the servant waited by a well where young women were collecting water. One of them, a girl named Rebecca, offered him a drink of water. The servant knew that this was a sign from God and that Rebecca should be Isaac's wife.

The servant told Rebecca his story, and she agreed to return with him to Canaan. Isaac fell in love with her, and they were soon married. In time they had twin boys—Esau and Jacob.

Jacob

Jacob was the son of Isaac and Rebecca.
His twin brother, Esau, had been born
first and was his father's favorite child.
But Rebecca loved Jacob very much.
When Isaac was an old man, Jacob
and Rebecca tricked him into giving
Jacob the blessing meant for the
firstborn. Esau was so angry
about this that Jacob ran away.
He traveled all day
and when the sun set,
he lay down to sleep,
resting his head
on a stone.

That night Jacob had a dream. He saw angels going up
and down a stairway between earth and Heaven. In the
dream God spoke to Jacob, saying, "I am the God
of Abraham and Isaac. The land on which you sleep
will be yours, and I will look after you wherever you go."

The next morning Jacob poured oil over the stone
that had been his pillow and dedicated the spot to God.
He promised God, "If you protect me, you will be my God."

Joseph

Joseph was the son of Jacob and his wife, Rachel. Jacob loved Joseph dearly and often spoiled him. This made his brothers jealous, so they sold him as a slave.

Joseph was taken to Egypt where he worked for Pharaoh. Although Joseph was honest, he ended up in prison. Here, with God's help, he interpreted the other prisoners' dreams.

One day Pharaoh had a puzzling dream—seven fat cows were eaten by seven thin cows. Pharaoh sent for Joseph who explained what the dream meant—there would be seven years of plenty and then seven years of famine. Pharaoh listened to Joseph and put him in charge of storing food.

Everything happened as Joseph had said. During the famine Joseph's family came to Egypt for food. Their descendants, the Israelites, settled there for many years.

Moses

Moses was the son of an Israelite woman. Many Israelites lived in Egypt, but their lives were hard because Pharaoh used them as slaves. One day, fearing that the Israelites might rise up against him, Pharaoh ordered all Israelite baby boys to be killed. Moses' mother put him in a basket among the reeds of the Nile River. There he was found by Pharaoh's daughter, who took him home.

Moses was brought up in Pharaoh's palace, but he always cared about the Israelites. In time God helped him rescue them from Egypt and lead them back to Canaan.

It was a long journey and as they passed Mount Sinai, God called Moses to the top of the mountain. There God gave him two tablets of stone on which the Ten Commandments were written. These were the laws that God wanted the Israelites to obey.

Joshua

Joshua was one of the Israelites who traveled out of Egypt with Moses. The journey lasted many years, and Moses grew old and frail. Before Moses died God guided him to choose Joshua as the Israelites' new leader.

When the Israelites finally reached Canaan, Joshua wanted to capture the city of Jericho, but it was surrounded by strong city walls. God told Joshua what to do, and he followed the instructions carefully.

On each of the following six days Joshua marched once around the city with his army and with seven priests. The priests carried trumpets made of rams' horns.

On the seventh day he marched his men around the city seven times. Then the priests blew on their trumpets, and the soldiers shouted loudly. Suddenly the mighty walls of Jericho crumbled to the ground.

Deborah

Deborah was a prophet who was chosen by God to help the Israelites during a difficult time. God's people had turned away from God, and their lives were very hard. They were treated cruelly by Jabin, the King of Canaan.

Deborah's task was to rescue the Israelites and help them return to God. Deborah did everything that God asked her to do. She sent for a man called Barak and asked him to gather an army of ten thousand men to fight King Jabin. Barak was willing to do this as long as Deborah agreed to help.

King Jabin's army had nine hundred chariots made of iron and was led by a great general called Sisera. But with God's help Barak and Deborah got the better of him. They forced Sisera and his men onto muddy ground where their chariots got stuck. Then they pushed his army into a narrow valley and defeated it. The Israelites were free at last.

Gideon

After many years of living in peace in Canaan the Israelites found themselves under attack from a people called the Midianites.

God sent an angel to a man called Gideon and told him to destroy the Midianites. Gideon was only a timid farmer, but he trusted God and immediately gathered up a huge army. God helped Gideon choose the best three hundred men to go into battle. Under the cover of night Gideon and his men made a surprise attack. They blew trumpets made of rams' horns and waved burning torches. The Midianites panicked and began to fight among themselves. The Israelites were soon victorious, and the victory was God's.

Samson

Samson was dedicated to God from birth. He was a strong and mighty warrior. He once killed a lion with his bare hands. The Philistines, the Israelites' greatest enemy, hated him.

Samson loved Delilah, a Philistine woman. She tried to discover the secret of his strength. When he told her that it lay in his hair, Delilah betrayed him and had it cut off. The Philistines seized Samson and blinded him and then threw him into prison.

Months later the Philistines held a banquet. They sent for Samson to make fun of him. By this time his hair had grown back. With a prayer to God, he pushed over two stone pillars so that the roof of the hall fell in. All the Philistines were killed and so was Samson.

Ruth and Naomi

Ruth lived in a place called Moab. She married a young Israelite who had traveled there with his family. Sadly he died along with his brother and father, leaving his mother, Naomi, alone in a foreign land.

Naomi decided to return to her hometown of Bethlehem. She told Ruth to go back to her own family, but Ruth loved Naomi and wanted to take care of her. She told Naomi, "Wherever you go I will go. Your people will be my people, and your God will be my God."

Back in Bethlehem life was hard. Ruth worked in the fields, collecting grain for food. The land was owned by a kind farmer named Boaz. Ruth and Boaz got married and had a son who many years later became the grandfather of David, Israel's greatest king.

Samuel

When Samuel was born, he was the answer to the prayers of his mother, Hannah. She had begged God to give her a son and had promised to offer his life to God. So when Samuel was still only a boy, Hannah sent him to the temple at Shiloh, and he became a servant to the priest Eli.

One night when Samuel was trying to get to sleep in the temple, he heard someone calling his name— once, twice, three times. He thought it was Eli calling, but Eli told him that the voice was God's. God told Samuel that he would become the priest at Shiloh after Eli died.

Samuel was always guided by God. He grew up to be a great priest and prophet, and everything he said turned out to be true. The Israelites trusted him so much that they asked him to choose a king for them. With God's help, Samuel chose Saul.

Saul

Saul was the first king of the Israelites. He was still only a young man when the prophet Samuel anointed him by pouring oil over his head. The ceremony was a sign that Saul had been chosen to be a future king.

At first Saul was a good king, but then he began to ignore God's wishes. In time God lost patience with him and told Samuel to look for a new king. Secretly, and with God's help, Samuel anointed a shepherd boy named David. He would be the next king.

David was a wonderful harp player, and when Saul heard him playing, he made David his personal servant. Saul loved David but soon became jealous of him. He tried to have David killed, but he never succeeded.

Eventually Saul died in battle, fighting the Philistines.

David

When David was a young shepherd boy, he was handsome and very brave. He made a slingshot and practiced firing stones so that he could defend his sheep against lions and bears.

At this time King Saul was fighting the Philistines. One of their soldiers was Goliath, a mighty giant who carried a huge sword and a spear as thick as a tree. Goliath challenged any Israelite to fight him. David trusted God, and so he volunteered.

He collected five pebbles from a stream, picked up his slingshot, and went to face Goliath. He told the giant, "Because I have God on my side, I have the power to kill you." And with one shot from his slingshot, he did just that.

Years later, after Saul died, David became king. He captured Jerusalem and made it the capital. He became Israel's greatest ruler.

Solomon

Solomon was the son of David and Bathsheba. He became king after David's death. He ruled over Israel for 40 years. During this time the country was at peace, and the people were happy and safe.

Early in Solomon's reign God spoke to him in a dream and offered him a gift. Solomon asked God for wisdom so that he could rule his people well. God was pleased with this answer, so he gave Solomon not only wisdom but riches and long life too.

Solomon built a great temple to God. It was made of the finest stone, wood, and precious metals, and it stood in the center of Jerusalem.

One day the Queen of Sheba heard about Solomon's fame and decided to visit him. When she saw his riches and wisdom, she praised God for loving Israel and for choosing such a fine king.

Elijah

Elijah was a prophet. He lived at a time when the Israelites were ruled by a wicked king named Ahab. One day Elijah spoke fearlessly to Ahab, telling him that God was angry and would punish him by sending a drought. Ahab was furious and did not believe a word Elijah said.

But the prophet's words turned out to be true. There was a drought, and food became scarce. God looked after Elijah, sending him to live in the wilderness next to a stream.

Each day God sent a flock of ravens to carry scraps of food to Elijah. In time the stream dried up, and God sent Elijah to a nearby town for shelter at a widow's house. All she had was a cup of flour and a few drops of olive oil. Yet the whole time Elijah stayed with her the food never ran out.

Elisha

Elisha was chosen by God to follow Elijah as a prophet. In his lifetime Elisha performed many miracles, and one of these took place in the city of Shunem. There was a woman who always welcomed Elisha and gave him a room for the night. One day he wanted to thank her for her kindness, and so he told her that she would have a child. She was overjoyed when twelve months later she gave birth to a son.

But her joy was short-lived. When the boy was still very young, he suddenly became sick and died. She lay his lifeless body on Elisha's bed and then set off to find the prophet. Elisha returned with her at once to Shunem. He knelt beside the child's body and prayed for him.

All at once the boy grew warm and—achoo!—he suddenly sneezed. Miracle of miracles—the child was alive!

Jonah

Jonah was a prophet. One day God told him to go to the city of Nineveh where the people were breaking God's laws. Jonah had to tell them to change their ways. But he didn't want to go, so he boarded a ship to get away.

Out at sea there was a horrible storm. Jonah knew that it was punishment from God for his disobedience. He told the crew to throw him overboard. The moment they did the wind dropped, and the sea grew calm.

Jonah thought he was going to drown, but then a great fish swallowed him. He spent three days and three nights inside the fish, and then he was spit out near the shore. Jonah thanked God he was still alive! He went straight to Nineveh. He warned the people to obey God's laws or they would be destroyed. The people listened to him and were sorry. They returned to God.

Isaiah

Isaiah was a great prophet, but there was a time when he thought he wasn't good enough to be one of God's messengers. "I am a sinful man," he said. Soon after an angel visited him and told him that his sins had been forgiven.

During the time of Isaiah the Israelites were slaves to the king of Assyria, and their lives were very hard. Many of them felt so hopeless that they turned away from God. Isaiah told them that God was angry, and the future would be even worse if they disobeyed God's laws.

Isaiah was a great speaker, and as well as blaming his people he also tried to comfort and inspire them. He told them that Israel would be great again. He said that one day a baby would be born who would grow up to be a great leader. Isaiah called this leader the Messiah and told the people that he would bring peace to everyone on earth. By talking about a brighter future he gave his people hope.

Josiah

Josiah became king when he was just eight years old. His father and grandfather had been king before him, but they had disobeyed God. Under them the people had worshiped false gods.

Josiah wanted his people to return to God. First he got rid of the false priests and destroyed their statues and altars. Next he began to rebuild Solomon's temple, which had fallen into disrepair. During the work a priest discovered some ancient books. They contained the Ten Commandments—the laws that God gave to Moses.

Josiah read the laws to his people, and as he spoke his face grew pale. He knew that his people had broken these laws and faced a fearful punishment. Josiah promised to obey God's laws all his life. For this God did not punish the people until the king died.

Jeremiah

Jeremiah was a prophet who lived in Jerusalem when many people were wicked and selfish. They worshiped false gods and were heartless to the poor.

Jeremiah knew that God was angry, and he warned the people of the danger ahead. He told them that they would be severely punished unless they changed their ways. But the people attacked and beat him and refused to listen to what he said.

Poor Jeremiah—he trusted God and knew that his words would come true. He said that Jerusalem would be attacked and captured, and the people would become slaves. His words angered the king, who threw Jeremiah into a dark, muddy well. But some days later he was rescued by friends who pulled him out with ropes. Jeremiah survived to see his prophecies come true.

Shadrach

Shadrach and his two friends Meshach and Abednego worked at the royal court in the kingdom of Babylon. One day the king, Nebuchadnezzar, built a huge golden statue and ordered everyone to bow down to it. Those who did not would be burned alive.

Shadrach, Meshach, and Abednego worshiped the God of Israel, so they refused to bow down to this false idol. Nebuchadnezzar ordered them to be thrown into a furnace. As the king watched he saw that the flames didn't harm them. To his amazement he saw a fourth figure standing next to them— it was an angel sent by God to protect the men from harm. The king instantly freed the men and ordered everyone to respect the God of Israel.

Daniel

When Jerusalem was attacked by the Babylonians, Daniel was taken to Babylon to work at the royal court. He was a good worker, and in time he became a minister to King Darius.

Some people were jealous of Daniel's success. Knowing that he prayed to the God of Israel, they persuaded Darius to pass a new law. It ordered that no one should pray to any god or man but only to the king. Those who disobeyed this law would be thrown into a lions' den.

But Daniel would pray to no one but God. His enemies caught him and took him to the king. Darius was upset at the thought of losing Daniel, but he had to obey the law. That evening Daniel was thrown into a lions' den.

The next morning, to everyone's amazement, Daniel was safe and sound. An angel had protected him all night long. Darius was overjoyed. He rounded up Daniel's enemies and threw them to the lions instead.

Ezekiel

Ezekiel was a priest and a prophet. Like many of the other Israelites he had been taken to Babylon after the capture of Jerusalem. The news from their homeland was very bad—Solomon's temple had been destroyed, and Jerusalem lay in ruins. The Israelites were in despair.

Ezekiel wanted to comfort the people and give them hope, so he told them about a vision he once had. God had shown him a valley full of bones. Ezekiel told the bones that God could breathe new life into them. As he spoke there was a great rattling sound— all the bones joined together and were covered in flesh.

Ezekiel explained to the Israelites that they could be like these bones. If they were good and obeyed God's laws, God would give them back their freedom and their land—in other words, their lives.

Nehemiah and Ezra

Nehemiah and Ezra helped the Israelites after their return to Jerusalem. The people faced a difficult time, and parts of the city were still in ruins. Nehemiah wanted to help by rebuilding the city walls. One night he visited the ruins and decided what repairs were needed. It was a huge job, but Nehemiah inspired the Israelites,

and the work was finished quickly.

Nehemiah restored the Israelites' city, but it was Ezra who restored their faith. A scholar and a priest, he understood all of the laws that God had given Moses. Many of the Israelites had forgotten these laws, so Ezra called everyone together and explained them from beginning to end—it took him about eight hours! The entire city felt pure and whole again and ready to make a new start.

Esther

Esther was a beautiful Jewish woman who lived in Persia. One day Xerxes, the king of Persia, decided to make her his queen. He thought she was Persian, but Esther was a Jew.

King Xerxes had a minister named Haman who wanted everyone to bow down to him. Esther's cousin Mordecai refused because he was also a Jew and would only bow down to God. Haman decided to punish Mordecai and every Jew in Persia. He went to Xerxes and tricked the king into agreeing to kill the Jews.

Mordecai asked Queen Esther to beg her husband for mercy. She was very frightened but agreed to try. She invited Xerxes and Haman to a wonderful dinner and then told the king about his wicked minister's plans. Bravely she begged her husband to spare her life and those of her people.

Xerxes loved Esther and wanted her to be happy. He saw how Haman had tried to trick him, so he sent Haman to his death.

Job

Job was a wealthy farmer.
He was a good man who
worked hard, cared for
his family, and faithfully
worshiped God. But one
day everything changed.
He lost his animals, his
children were killed,
and boils appeared
all over his body.

Job wondered why
he was being punished this way. His three friends tried
to explain it—he must have done something wrong.
Job knew this was not true and begged God to tell
him why he, an innocent man, should suffer.

Suddenly out of a whirlwind God spoke to Job,
"Who dares challenge my wisdom and power?
Where were you when I made the world, Job?"

When Job heard these words, he understood that
God was all-powerful. He should simply have faith
in God. This pleased God so much that Job was blessed
with a new family, great wealth, and a long life.

Mary

Mary lived in Nazareth in Galilee and was engaged to a carpenter named Joseph. One day the angel Gabriel visited her and told her that she would have a baby who would be the Son of God. Mary was amazed but put her trust in God.

Months later, when the baby was due, an order went out telling everyone to go to their birthplace so they could register to pay taxes. So Mary and Joseph loaded a donkey and traveled to Bethlehem in Judea.

When they arrived, the town was so busy that they could find nowhere to stay. An innkeeper offered them a stable. That night Mary gave birth to a baby boy. She called him Jesus and placed him in a manger. Later some shepherds came to visit Jesus. An angel had told them about his birth.

Simeon and Anna

Simeon was a very old, very holy man who lived in the city of Jerusalem. He had been promised by God that before he died he would see the Messiah—the leader who Isaiah had prophesied would save Israel and the world.

One day Simeon was visiting the temple when Mary and Joseph brought in baby Jesus to be blessed. Simeon knew instantly that this was the Messiah. He took Jesus in his arms and praised and thanked God. "He will be like a light, guiding the people of Israel and of every nation of the world," Simeon said.

A prophet named Anna was also in the temple. She was very old and spent most of her time fasting and worshiping God. Anna, too, recognized Jesus as the Messiah. She was overjoyed, and after thanking God she began to spread the news around Jerusalem.

Herod

At the time when Jesus was born Herod was the governor of Judea. He was a clever, ruthless man who enjoyed power.

One day he was visited by wise men from the East. They told him that they were following a star. It would lead them to a baby who had been born in Bethlehem and who would one day become king of the Jews. They were carrying presents for the baby—gold, frankincense, and myrrh.

Herod was worried—he did not want a new king growing up in his land. He asked the wise men to come back and tell him exactly where the child could be found.

The wise men were delighted when they found Jesus, but they were warned in a dream not to return to Herod.

Herod was furious when they failed to appear and ordered all the baby boys in Bethlehem to be killed. But an angel warned Joseph about the danger, and he led Mary and Jesus to safety in Egypt.

John the Baptist

John the Baptist was the son of Elizabeth and Zechariah, who had been warned of his birth by an angel. They were told that one day their son would be a prophet.

John grew up to be a remarkable man. He wore a rough shirt made of camel hair and ate nothing but locusts and honey. He was a powerful speaker, and huge crowds gathered to hear him. He told them that a great leader called the Messiah was coming and that they should prepare for him by being baptized. The ceremony of baptism could "wash away" their sins with water as long as these sins were truly confessed first.

One day Jesus came to be baptized in the Jordan River. He asked John to baptize him, and John did as he asked. When Jesus rose out of the water, a dove flew down and the voice of God was heard, saying, "This is my beloved son in whom I am very pleased."

Jairus

Jairus was an important man in the synagogue of Capernaum. One day he went to Jesus, begging him to heal his young daughter who was dangerously sick. Jesus agreed.

As the two men went on their way a sick woman struggled through the crowd that had gathered to see Jesus. She managed to touch Jesus' cloak, and instantly she felt well again. Jesus turned to face her. "It is your faith in God that has made you well," he said.

Then Jesus and Jairus hurried on. Soon they heard news that the girl had died, but Jesus told Jairus, "Only believe and your daughter will be well."

When they arrived at Jairus' house, Jesus took the dead girl's hands and commanded her to get up. Immediately she opened her eyes. Jairus' daughter was healed.

Lazarus

Lazarus and his two sisters, Martha and Mary, lived near Jerusalem in the town of Bethany. They were all good friends of Jesus.

One day Jesus heard that Lazarus was very sick. He traveled to Bethany, but by the time he arrived Lazarus had been dead for four days. Martha and Mary were weeping for their brother. "If only you had been here sooner," they said to Jesus, "Lazarus would not have died." Jesus tried to comfort them. He said that Lazarus would live again and told them to have faith in God.

Jesus made his way to the tomb where Lazarus had been laid. He ordered the stone at the entrance of the tomb to be rolled away. Then he called to Lazarus, commanding him to come outside. Moments later Lazarus appeared alive and well, wearing his burial clothes. This was one of the most amazing miracles that Jesus ever performed.

Jesus

Jesus is the Son of God. He came to earth as the Messiah to bring about God's kingdom. He was helped in his work by twelve trusted friends, the disciples.

Jesus was a wonderful teacher and told simple stories called parables. He urged people to love their enemies, and he reached out to tax collectors, lepers, and criminals, who were unpopular at that time.

Jesus performed many miracles. Once after hours of preaching to a crowd of people, he realized that everyone was hungry. The only person with any food was a young boy who had five small loaves of bread and two fish. Jesus took the food and prayed to God. Then he gave it to his disciples to pass around. There was enough to feed over 5,000 people.

That same evening there was another miracle. The disciples were rowing across the Lake of Galilee when a storm began. They were afraid their boat would sink. They suddenly saw a figure coming toward them, walking on the water. It was Jesus. As soon as the disciple Peter recognized his master, he

jumped out of the boat and began to walk toward him. Moments later he became scared and started sinking. Jesus reached out and pulled him up, telling him to have more faith.

Not everybody trusted Jesus. Some of the things he said and did shocked and offended people— especially priests, Jewish elders, and Roman rulers. They thought he was a troublemaker, and they had him arrested and crucified.

Three days after his crucifixion, Jesus rose from the dead. Several weeks later he ascended into Heaven and returned to God, his Father. His work on earth was done.

Bartimaeus

Bartimaeus was a blind beggar. Every day he sat by the side of the road that led out of Jericho and begged from the passersby.

One day Jesus was leaving the city. As usual he was surrounded by a crowd, eager to speak to him and hear what he said. When Bartimaeus heard that Jesus was nearby, he started to call out his name. This annoyed many of the people in the crowd, and they tried to keep him quiet. But he ignored them and kept on shouting, "Jesus, have mercy on me."

Jesus heard him and asked the people to bring Bartimaeus over. When they were face to face, Jesus asked Bartimaeus what it was that he wanted. Bartimaeus replied, "I want to see." Jesus saw that his faith was very strong and instantly healed his sight. Bartimaeus was delighted. He praised Jesus and joined the crowd that was following him.

Zacchaeus

Zacchaeus was a rich tax collector. Nobody liked him because he was a crook and cheated people out of their money.

One day Zacchaeus heard that Jesus was passing by. There was a big crowd lining the road, and Zacchaeus, who was very short, climbed a nearby fig tree to get a better view.

Soon Jesus came along. As he passed beneath the tree he looked up at Zacchaeus and said, "Hurry down. I want to rest at your house for a while." At this the crowd began to grumble—it was wrong for Jesus to visit the house of such a sinful man. But Zacchaeus spoke up, saying he was sorry for his sins. He promised to return four times the money he had stolen and give half his riches to the poor.

Jesus was pleased. He explained to the crowd that it was people like Zacchaeus that he had come to save.

The Twelve Disciples

Jesus had many followers. He chose twelve of them to be his trusted friends and to help him with his work. They were James and his brother John, Peter, Andrew, Matthew, Philip, Simon, Bartholomew, Thomas, James, Thaddeus, and Judas Iscariot.

The twelve disciples came from different walks of life. Four of them—James, John, Peter, and Andrew—were fishermen, and Matthew was a tax collector. They all left their jobs to follow Jesus because they were inspired by his words and deeds.

The more the disciples learned about Jesus, the more their faith in him grew. They believed he was the Messiah, and they saw him perform many miracles.

One night Peter, James, and John saw Jesus shining brightly in the presence of the great prophets Moses and Elijah. Then they heard God call him "my Son."

During the last week of Jesus' life there was a special Jewish festival called Passover. Jesus celebrated it by eating with his disciples in Jerusalem. It was to be their last supper together. Jesus told them that one of them would betray him to his enemies. He said, "The one I give this bread to will be the traitor." He handed the bread to Judas.

The next day Judas led Roman soldiers to a garden where Jesus was praying and identified him with a kiss. The soldiers led Jesus away.

The disciples were greatly saddened by Jesus' death, but they continued to preach and tell people about his life.

Pontius Pilate

Pontius Pilate was the Roman governor of Judea. After Jesus was arrested in Jerusalem he was sent to Pilate for trial.

Jesus' enemies wanted him put to death. They said he was guilty of breaking Jewish law and of claiming to be king. Pilate questioned Jesus but decided he was harmless. He suggested that Jesus should be released, but the crowd disagreed. They wanted a murderer named Barabbas to be freed instead. So with a heavy heart Pilate handed Jesus over to be crucified.

Jesus was stripped, and a crown of thorns was put upon his head. He had to carry a heavy wooden cross through the streets and was jeered and mocked by the crowd. At the place of crucifixion he was nailed to the cross. At midday the sky overhead grew dark. Three hours later Jesus died.

Joseph of Arimathea

Joseph, who came from Arimathea, a town not far from Jerusalem, was an important and wealthy man. He was a member of the Jewish high court, but he was also a follower of Jesus. He kept this a secret from other Jews because the Jewish high court hated Jesus and all of his followers.

After Jesus had died Joseph went to see Pontius Pilate and asked for Jesus' body. Pilate agreed. Then Joseph and his friend Nicodemus, who was another follower of Jesus, took the body down from the wooden cross. They rubbed it with oils and wrapped it in a linen sheet. Then they laid the body in Joseph's own family tomb—an empty cave recently dug out of the solid rock. Before they walked away they rolled a huge, heavy stone across the entrance of the tomb.

51

Mary Magdalene

Mary Magdalene was a friend and follower of Jesus. She hadn't always lived a good life, but with Jesus' help she had made a fresh start. She followed Jesus devotedly and was near him when he died on the cross.

Two days after Jesus' crucifixion Mary visited his tomb. But when she got there she discovered that the tomb was empty, and the stone had been rolled away.

Mary ran to get the disciples Peter and John, who came to see the tomb for themselves. They ran away, talking excitedly, and left Mary weeping by the tomb.

Soon a man came up to comfort her. She thought he was just the gardener, but when he spoke her name she realized it was Jesus! Jesus told Mary he had risen from the dead and would soon return to God in Heaven.

Cleopas

Cleopas was a follower of Jesus. A few days after Jesus' death Cleopas and a friend were walking to a village called Emmaus, talking about Jesus' arrest and crucifixion. On the road they were joined by Jesus, but as strange as it sounds neither man recognized him. They all walked along together. Jesus asked why the men looked so sad. They told him all about Jesus and the heartbreaking news of his death. Jesus tried to comfort them, saying that the Messiah had to die, just as the prophets had foretold.

When the three men reached Emmaus, they decided to eat together. Jesus picked up some bread, broke it, and blessed it—and suddenly his companions knew who he was! At that very moment Jesus disappeared. The two men were astounded but overjoyed. They rushed back to Jerusalem to find the disciples and tell them what they had seen.

The Holy Spirit

After Jesus had ascended into Heaven to return to God, his Father, the disciples went to Jerusalem. Jesus had told them to go to the city and wait to be baptized—not with water but with the Holy Spirit.

The Holy Spirit was God's special gift. The Spirit would fill them with power, allowing them to take God's message to everyone— whoever or wherever they might be.

At this time of year there was a special Jewish festival known as the Feast of Pentecost. The disciples gathered together, praying and waiting. Suddenly they felt a strong wind blowing, and it filled the entire room. Then tongues of flame came down and touched each and every one of them. For the disciples it was an amazing feeling— the breath of God, the coming of the Spirit.

When it was over, they found that
they could speak many other languages.
Now they could travel and tell people
the good news that God loved them
and would forgive their sins.
Filled with this new power,
they went out into the city and
spoke to great crowds of people.
In time they found they had
the power to heal just as
Jesus had done.
This power came
from the Holy Spirit.
The disciples could now
go out and do whatever
God wanted them to do.
It was as if Jesus was there
in person again. But now
his power was shared among
them all, allowing others
to learn and be helped by God.
With the power of the Holy Spirit
every believer could know God
and live life according to God's way.

Stephen

Stephen was chosen by the disciples to help them spread the message of Jesus. After listening to the disciples some Jewish people believed that Jesus Christ was the Messiah. These people became known as Christians. But many Jewish people did not believe this and became angry with the Christians.

Stephen was a great speaker and encouraged many people to become Christians. He explained the meaning of Jesus' death and resurrection. He said that Jesus died to save people from their sins and rose again to show his power over death. People who believed in him would have eternal life. This shocked the Jewish leaders, who took Stephen to the Jewish high court. There he had a vision of God and Jesus. This so angered the court that they ordered him to be stoned to death. In this way Stephen became the first Christian martyr.

Dorcas

Dorcas was a Christian woman who lived in the town of Joppa. She was kind and helpful to the poor. One day she became gravely sick and died soon afterward. Her friends were shocked and heartbroken. When they heard that Peter, the disciple of Jesus, was visiting a nearby town, they decided to send for him.

Peter came to Dorcas' house and knelt beside her bed. He prayed for a moment, and then raising his head, he told her to get up. Amazingly she opened her eyes, sat up, and looked around. She was alive! Her friends were amazed and overjoyed. They spread news of the miracle throughout the town. Many people who heard Dorcas' story became believers and asked to be baptized.

Paul

Paul, who was first named Saul, was a Jew who followed his religion very strictly. He did not believe that Jesus was the Messiah, and he hated the Christians. He wanted to stamp out their new religion, and he had many of them arrested.

One day he was traveling to the city of Damascus when he was blinded by a bright light. He heard the voice of Jesus ask, "Saul, why are you persecuting me?"

From that moment Saul was blind. He was led into Damascus, and he waited there for three days. Then Jesus sent one of his followers to restore his sight. Saul realized that Jesus was truly the Messiah, and he was immediately baptized. From that day forward he was known as Paul.

People were amazed by Paul's change of heart. He became the most important missionary of the new Christian church. He traveled tirelessly, spreading the word of Jesus far and wide to places such as Italy, Turkey, and Greece.

Silas

Silas was a Christian and a friend of Paul, and he traveled with him on many journeys. It was dangerous work being a Christian missionary because sometimes they were seen as troublemakers.

One day when they were in Philippi, a city in Greece, Silas and Paul were beaten and thrown into prison. Despite this the two men were strong and calm, and they prayed and sang to God.

That night there was an earthquake in the city. The prison doors burst open, and the prisoners' chains fell from the walls. The jailer was terrified that his prisoners had escaped and that he would be blamed. But Paul called out that they were both still there, and that they would not try to escape. This greatly relieved the jailer. He could feel some power in Paul and Silas and asked to be baptized. The following day an order arrived, and the two missionaries were set free.

Timothy

Timothy was a close friend of Paul. He had a Greek father and a Jewish mother, but after listening to Paul he decided to become a Christian. After that he traveled widely with Paul and helped him with his missionary work.

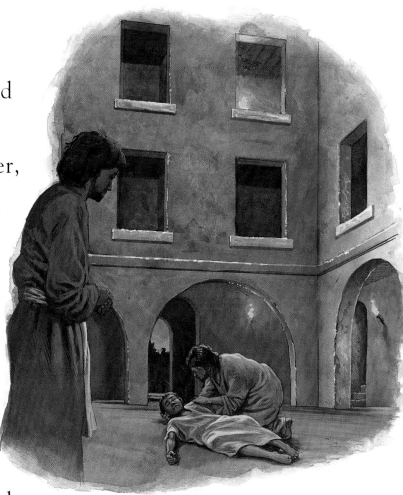

One day while they were on their travels Paul preached to a roomful of people. He spoke for a very long time, continuing into the night. A young man called Eutychus, who had been trying to stay awake, fell asleep by an open window and toppled out to his death. Timothy watched as Paul rushed downstairs and cradled Eutychus in his arms. Instantly the young man came back to life.

Timothy also went on journeys of his own, spreading the word of Jesus. He was timid at first, but Paul wrote to him often, encouraging him and praising his faith. To Paul he was like a son—someone who would carry on his work.

Luke

Luke was a doctor and a good friend of Paul and helped him when he was in trouble. Paul was often accused by Jewish elders of preaching against their law. Time after time they had him arrested. At last he was sent to Rome to be judged by the emperor himself. Luke decided to travel with him.

During the voyage their ship ran into a terrible storm, and the crew feared for their lives. Paul comforted them, saying that an angel had told him everyone would be safe.

Soon the ship hit a sandbank and began to break up in the storm. Although they were still a long way from land Luke, Paul, and every crew member had to leap into the towering waves. Some clung to wooden planks, and others swam for the shore. But everyone escaped alive—not a single person drowned.

Index

Main entries
are in **bold**.

Glossary

anoint	to make something or someone holy by pouring oil over it
ascension	Jesus' return from earth to his Father in Heaven
baptize	to plunge someone in water as a sign of sin washed away
bless	to ask for God's help and protection for someone
Christians	people who believe that Jesus Christ is the Messiah—the person chosen by God—and who try to follow his teachings
crucify	to kill someone by nailing them to a wooden cross
disciple	one of twelve close followers of Jesus; sometimes called an apostle
fast	to go without food
Pentecost	a Jewish festival that celebrates the harvest and the giving of the Ten Commandments
Israelites	people who lived in Israel and who were descended from Abraham, Isaac, and Jacob
Jews	the Israelites who followed God's commandments but did not think that Jesus was the Messiah
martyr	someone who is killed because of their Christian beliefs
missionary	a person who teaches others about his or her religion
persecute	to treat someone cruelly and unfairly
Pharaoh	the ruler, or king, of Egypt
Philistines	a strong, warlike group who attacked and fought the Israelites
preach	to talk to people in order to give them religious advice
priest	a person chosen and trained to lead religious services
prophesy	to say what will happen in the future
prophet	someone who receives messages from God and tells other people about them
resurrection	Jesus' return from death to a new life that lasts forever
sacrifice	an offering made to God
synagogue	a Jewish place of worship, study, and meeting